How to Live in

Divine Blessings

Brother Charles, A vessel of God

HOW TO LIVE IN GOD'S DIVINE BLESSINGS

Scripture quotations marked NIV are taken from the Holy Bible, New International Version®. NIV®. Copyright © 1973, 1978, 1984 by International Bible Society. Used by permission of Zondervan. All rights reserved. [Biblica]

iUniverse books may be ordered through booksellers or by contacting:

iUniverse
1663 Liberty Drive
Bloomington, IN 47403
www.iuniverse.com
844-349-9409

Because of the dynamic nature of the Internet, any web addresses or links contained in this book may have changed since publication and may no longer be valid. The views expressed in this work are solely those of the author and do not necessarily reflect the views of the publisher, and the publisher hereby disclaims any responsibility for them.

Author Contact Info:
BrotherCharlesA@gmail.com

ISBN: 978-1-6632-2887-1 (sc)
ISBN: 978-1-6632-2888-8 (e)

Library of Congress Control Number: 2021919467

Print information available on the last page.

iUniverse rev. date: 09/21/2021

Contents

Introduction

Most Christians are constantly searching for God's blessings. Some are moving from one church to another, hoping to find a place of worship where God's blessings reside. Many have made mistakes along the way. What they fail to realize is that blessing is part of the nature of God. This means you ought not to be searching for God's blessings if you are a follower of Jesus Christ, for you are already blessed. Proverbs 10:6 (New International Version) tells us that "blessings crown the head of the righteous, but violence overwhelms the mouth of the wicked." And who are the righteous? The righteous are the followers of Jesus.

There is a distinctive difference between the pre-and post-Adamic era from the perspective of God's blessings. God did not attach any condition when He blessed man after the creation (Genesis 1:26) because man was created in the image of God. God instructed man not to eat from the tree of the knowledge of good and evil; God told them that they would die the day they do so (Genesis 2:17). Man disobeyed God's instruction after being deceived by the devil (Genesis 3:1–6). This disobedience was what created the separation between God and man.

This separation introduced conditions to God's blessings. Because blessings are part of God's nature, we would have to get rid of our sinful nature in order to receive from God. An act of self-righteousness cannot qualify us, making this a challenging feat to attain. God, out of His infinite mercy, compassion, and love, made a provision for us. It's only through this provision that you and I can be restored to God's original plan.

This book covers the conditions that are attached to God's blessings. Questions like, "How do we meet these conditions?" and, "How do we enable the manifestation of God's blessings?" and a whole lot more are answered in detail.

Chapter 1

As a Christian, you are supposed to "trust in the Lord with all your heart and lean not on your own understanding; in all your ways submit to him, and he will make your paths straight." (Proverbs 3:5–6). In Psalm 37:23, the Bible tells us that "the Lord makes firm the step of the one who delights in him." God made this so since the beginning of time. There is nothing we can do to change this; either we let Him guide our steps, or we do it ourselves. The problem with doing it ourselves is that it makes it difficult for us to walk with Him. There is no way we can walk with God if we are the ones calling the shots. Our course is of the Lord; in Him, we live and move and have our being (Acts 17:28).

Here is what the Bible has to say on this same subject in Matthew 6:33, "but seek first his kingdom and his righteousness, and all these things will be given to you as well." All these things include food, clothing, shelter, and so on. If God can be so kind to feed the birds of the air, which neither sow nor reap nor gather into barns, how much more us, who He created in His image! (Matthew 6:26).

Being created in the image of God makes us very special to Him. This explains why God gave us dominion over every living thing that moves on the earth. It was God's desire for us to subdue the earth, to be fruitful, and to multiply from the beginning of time (Genesis 1:28). You can't be created in the image of God and not showcase His nature.

God wants us to do well on earth as was revealed to us in 3 John 1:2, "Dear friend, I pray that you may enjoy good health and that all may go well with you, even as your soul is getting along well." This Bible passage reaffirms the notion that it's God's desire for us to live a successful life. In case you are still in doubt, here is what the Bible has to say about this same topic in Psalm 8:4–9, "what is mankind that you are mindful of them, human beings that you care for them? You have made them a little lower than the angels and crowned them with glory and honor. You made them rulers over the works of your hands; you put everything under their feet: all flocks and herds, and the animals of the wild, the birds in the sky, and the fish in the sea, all that swim the paths of the seas. LORD, our Lord, how majestic is your name in all the earth!"

I want you to ponder on this Word for a minute: "for You have crowned him with glory and honor." This is the life that God has called you into; that is, a life filled with glory and honor. God did not bring you into this world to be confused and lost. Nor did He bring you here to feel very miserable about yourself. "But you are a chosen people, a royal priesthood, a holy nation, God's special possession, that you may declare the praises of him who called you out of darkness into his wonderful light. Once you were not a people, but now you are the people of God; once you had not received mercy, but now you have received mercy." (1 Peter 2:9–10).

What Are God's Blessings?

God's blessings are supernatural provisions from God and are bestowed upon humans through a spoken Word. Most people mistake God's blessings for material things only, while others equate God's blessings to tangible items. God's blessings go beyond wealth; they include fruits of the womb, promotion, success in life, protection, peace, joy, favor, and happiness. The fact that you can't see joy, peace, favor, and happiness does not mean they don't exist. They are all part of God's blessings for us. Here is what the Bible has to say about joy and peace in Romans 15:13: "May the God of hope fill you with all joy and peace as you trust in him, so that you may overflow with hope by the power of the Holy Spirit."

As you can see from the above passage, in his letter to the disciples in Rome, apostle Paul prayed for them to be filled with all joy, not some joy. This is a powerful revelation on its own. He also wants them to be filled with peace in believing. Here is what Jesus has to say about peace in John 14:27: "Peace I leave with you; my peace I give you. I do not give to you as the world gives. Do not let your hearts be troubled, and do not be afraid." A mind that is not at peace with God will always be vulnerable to the enemy's attack. We are told to guide our mind, for life issues flow from it (Proverbs 4:23).

God's blessings are all-inclusive; they can't be separated. The Bible tells us in Proverbs 10:22 that "The blessing of the Lord brings wealth without painful toil for it." God's presence is life because that's who God is. Everything comes alive before Him who created Heaven and earth, and without whom nothing was made that was made. Even the dead and forgotten things can be brought back to life by our Maker.

Abrahamic Covenant

The Abrahamic covenant serves as the beginning of God's reconciliatory mission with man after the Adamic fall. Genesis 12:1–5:

"The LORD had said to Abram, "Go from your country, your people, and your father's household to the land I will show you.

²"I will make you into a great nation,
    and I will bless you;
I will make your name great,
    and you will be a blessing.
³I will bless those who bless you, and whoever curses you
    I will curse;
and all peoples on earth
    will be blessed through you."

⁴So Abram went, as the LORD had told him, and Lot went with him. Abram was seventy-five years old when he set out from Harran. ⁵He took his wife Sarai, his nephew

Lot, all the possessions they had accumulated and the people they had acquired in Harran, and they set out for the land of Canaan, and they arrived there."

Here is why God chose Abraham, Genesis 18:19, "For I have chosen him, so that he will direct his children and his household after him to keep the way of the LORD by doing what is right and just, so that the LORD will bring about for Abraham what he has promised him." It's important to note the Word "spoken," as this supports the notion that God's blessing comes from a spoken Word.

Our role as believers of the gospel of Jesus Christ is to receive and act on the Word. Doing so produces faith; here is what Hebrews 11:1-3 has to say about faith, "Now faith is confidence in what we hope for and assurance about what we do not see. This is what the ancients were commended for. By faith we understand that the universe was formed at God's command, so that what is seen was not made out of what was visible." It is also essential to know that it's impossible to please God without faith; faith is required for anyone who wants to receive from God.

Romans 4:3, "What does Scripture say? "Abraham believed God, and it was credited to him as righteousness." The Scripture tells us that wages are counted as debt for workers, meaning a worker is worthy of his reward. This was not the case with Abraham because God wanted His covenant with Abraham to be based on faith as such grace was made available for him by God. Why? So that he might be the father of those who believe. The Bible goes on to tell us in Romans 4:13–14, "It was not through the law that Abraham and his offspring received the promise that he would be heir of the world, but through the righteousness that comes by faith. For if those who depend on the law are heirs, faith means nothing, and the promise is worthless."

Redemption through Christ Jesus

The fall of man in Genesis 3:1–14, brought about the separation between man and God. This separation stalled God's divine blessings from manifesting in the lives of humans until God made a covenant with Abraham. The Abrahamic covenant was a precursor to the coming of Christ, who will later restore humans to God's original plan. "For he chose us in him before the creation of the world to be holy and blameless in his sight." (Ephesians 1:4). Being an all-knowing God, God knew before the creation of the world that humans would sin against Him at some point in time. As a result of this, Jesus was made to be a sacrificial lamb for us.

We cannot partake in God's divine blessings without being cleansed from our unrighteousness. Our unrighteousness prevents us from experiencing God's provisions, and it also cuts us off from our Maker. This is why and how Jesus came into the picture. The Bible tells us in John 3:16–17, "For God so loved the world that he gave his one and only Son, that whoever believes in him shall not perish but have eternal life."

Chapter 2

How to Receive God's Divine Blessings

Salvation

Salvation is the deliverance from sin and its consequences. It is the first step for those who want to partake in God's divine blessings. Humans cannot attain salvation without the acceptance of Christ in exchange for their sins. The journey of every Christian begins here. An act of self-righteousness cannot deliver us from our sin. Romans

3:23 states that, "For all have sinned and fall short of the glory of God."

The sin that's being referred to here was the one that was committed by our forefather Adam in the garden of Eden. Here is what the Bible has to say about this in the book of Romans 5:12, "Therefore, just as sin entered the world through one man, and death through sin, and in this way, death came to all people because all sinned." And in Romans 5:17, the Bible has this to say, "For if, by the trespass of the one man, death reigned through that one man, how much more will those who receive God's abundant provision of grace and of the gift of righteousness reign in life through the one man, Jesus Christ!"

Jesus is the propitiation for our sin. He was chosen by His Father before the foundation of this world to be a sacrificial lamb for man. He is the only way to the Father; Jesus is the sole heir to Abrahamic blessings. Here is what the Bible has to say about this: "So in Christ Jesus, you are all children of God through faith, for all of you who were baptized into Christ have clothed yourselves with Christ. There is neither Jew nor Gentile, neither slave nor free, nor is there male and female, for you are all one in Christ Jesus. If you belong to Christ, then you

are Abraham's seed, and heirs according to the promise."
(Galatians 3:26–29).

Jesus Christ became a curse for us when He was hanged
on a tree. Doing so redeemed us from the curse of the law.
It was part of the Roman tradition to hang condemned
criminals on the cross (crucifixion). Jesus chose to be
hanged on a tree for you and me because it is only by
doing so that you and I will become free from Adamic
sin and curse (Galatians 3:13).

It is worth knowing that you and I have been blessed with
every spiritual blessing in Christ Jesus (Ephesians 1:3).
You ought not to be asking God for something that He
has already given to you. What you need to do is accept
the gift, thank Him for it, and praise Him daily. This is
how we grow in faith. Remember that faith is a must for
all believers; it is impossible to please God without it.

How Do I Accept Jesus into My Life?

The first step towards accepting Jesus into your life is to
admit that you are a sinner, "For all have sinned and fall
short of the glory of God" (Romans 3:23). The second
step is to believe that Jesus died for you. Here is what the
Bible has to say about this in Romans 10:9–13:

"If you declare with your mouth, "Jesus is Lord," and believe in your heart that God raised him from the dead, you will be saved. For it is with your heart that you believe and are justified, and it is with your mouth that you profess your faith and are saved. As Scripture says, "Anyone who believes in him will never be put to shame." For there is no difference between Jew and Gentile—the same Lord is Lord of all and richly blesses all who call on him, for, "Everyone who calls on the name of the Lord will be saved."

The third step is to invite Jesus into your heart to become your Lord and personal Savior through prayer.

Here is the definition of prayer in case you are wondering what prayer is or how to pray. Prayer is a communion with God; that is, it is an interaction with God. It can be done any time of the day, although it's advisable to start and end your day with prayers. A prayerless Christian is a powerless Christian. Here is how Jesus taught His disciples to pray:

"This, then, is how you should pray: "'Our Father in Heaven, hallowed be your name, your kingdom come, your will be done, on earth as it is in Heaven. Give us today our daily bread. And forgive us our debts, as we also have forgiven our debtors. And lead us not into temptation, but deliver us from the evil one." (Matthew 6:9–13).

Prayer for Repentance

Here is how you implement the three steps together in prayer:

> Dear Jesus, I admit that I am a sinner. I repent and ask for Your forgiveness today. I believe that You died for me on the cross of Calvary to save me. I accept You as my Lord and personal Savior. Come into my life, Lord Jesus; I promise to serve You for the rest of my life. Help me to live right from this day onward. Amen!

The Importance of Prayer

The importance of prayer can be likened to communication between a child and their parents. Why? Because communication is a vital aspect of their relationship. If you exclude communication from their relationship, you are left with nothing. Communication is a necessary ingredient in the relationship between both parties. No communication means no directions or guidance from the parents to their child. It also means that there will be no verbal expressions of love and affection from the parents to their child at the initial stage and from the child to their parents later in life. Can you picture a child growing up in an environment where communication is missing? What do you think will become of that child? How about the parents? A good parent will never be happy under these conditions.

Prayer is how we communicate with God. We make our needs known to God through prayer. We also let God know how we feel about Him through prayer. Prayer enables us to ask God for direction and guidance at every step of the way.

Don't get into the habit of praying only when you are in need. God is not Santa Claus; He is your creator. Remember that He created you for fellowship.

Prayer is a necessary ingredient in the life of a believer. It is a must; prayer is the key. I cannot emphasize this enough: It is a requirement for every believer. You can never grow in your relationship with God if you don't pray regularly. The Bible tells us to pray without ceasing (1 Thessalonians 5:17).

Prayer can be used to change an unfavorable situation to a favorable one. The Bible made us to understand that: "Elijah was a human being, even as we are. He prayed earnestly that it would not rain, and it did not rain on the land for three and a half years. Again, he prayed, and the Heavens gave rain, and the earth produced its crops." (James 5:17–18)

Through prayer, we can access God's provisions for us. Prayer is a mighty weapon for God's children, the benefits of prayer are endless. Prayer can heal the sick and restore a broken home; prayer can restore a messed-up life or situation. With prayer, we can turn any situation around. Prayer is how we get God involved in things that we cannot handle ourselves. Prayer is paramount.

The Fear of God

The fact that you are saved by grace is not a license for you to continue to indulge in sin. Remember that you died to sin when you gave your life to Jesus Christ. Jesus destroyed the power of sin over your life when you surrendered your life to Him. "We were therefore buried with him through baptism into death in order that, just as Christ was raised from the dead through the glory of the Father, we too may live a new life." (Romans 6:4).

We can't continue to sin because we are under grace. Doing so will entangle us with the enemy, Satan. Sin makes it very challenging for us to work with God, much less to enjoy our relationship with Him. The actions we take as Christians determine the direction of our relationship with God. The more we draw closer to God, the more we are able to disentangle ourselves from those things that do not glorify God. You can't do this by your willpower; this is near to impossible. This is where having a Godly fear comes into play. The journey to having a Godly fear of God begins the moment we start spending time with God. Godly fear of God is the same as having a fear of God.

What is the fear of God? The fear of God is to eschew evil. Why? Because our God is holy. His eyes cannot withstand iniquities. You cannot serve a holy God with an iniquity-laden life. This is why Jesus was made a sacrificial lamb for us. The blood of Jesus cleansed us from every unrighteousness, which in return, enables us to become partakers of God's divine blessings.

We humans must do away with the works of the flesh: which include the following: sexual immorality, impurity, sensuality, anger, jealousy, and so on. We must embrace the fruits of the Spirit: love, joy, peace, kindness, gentleness, etc. (Galatians 5:22). Doing so is necessary; if we want to be successful in our walk with God. Part of being a born-again Christian involves changing one's way of life. We can't have it both ways. We need to let go of our old ways of life and embrace God's way of living as defined in the Bible.

Our minds must always be in God as we journey through life. It is by so doing that we can weather the storms of life. The fear of God keeps us from partaking in things that do not glorify Him. Joseph, when faced with temptation, chose not to sin against God. His fear of God kept him in check. He knew that fulfilling the wish of his master's wife would not only be a wrong thing to do against his master, who had shown him nothing but kindness but would also lead him to sin against God. So, he chose to walk away from the temptation (Genesis 39:8).

One interesting thing to note in the story of Joseph is that he was filled with God's divine blessings when he arrived in Potiphar's house. The Bible made us to understand that the Lord was with Joseph; as such, he became successful (Genesis 39:2–4). Joseph's master took note of God's favor in Joseph's life and made Joseph the overseer of his house and all that he had. So, you can imagine what would have become of Joseph had he succumbed to his master's wife's demand. Remember that Joseph was on a journey; the only one who knew how his journey would end was God.

Joseph did not blame God when he was incarcerated for a crime that he did not commit. Nor is there any information about him breaking down as a result of what happened to him. God was with Joseph in prison as He was with him when he served Potiphar. The prison keeper was quick to notice that God's favor was on the young man; as such, he gave him authority over all the prisoners' affairs.

Joseph's life in Egypt was something that God foreknew. It wasn't a coincidence that the king's officers were brought to the exact location where Joseph was kept. Here is what the Bible says in Proverbs 20:24: "A person's steps are directed by the LORD. How then can anyone understand their own way?" The fear of God is necessary for every believer who aspires to dwell in God's blessings. Joseph's action was what ushered him into the next level in his journey with God. We, as believers, need to take a clue from Joseph's action. We should try not to succumb to temptations no matter what. Sometimes these temptations show up when God is about to take us to a new level in our walk with Him. The Bible made us to understand that God would only teach the man who fears Him the way He, our creator, chose for that man. We are also told that such man would dwell in prosperity and that his descendant will inherit the earth. Finally, God's secret is with such people, as we saw in the life of Joseph.

Study the Word

Here is how the Bible defined the Word of God, "For the Word of God is alive and active. Sharper than any double-edged sword, it penetrates even to dividing soul and spirit, joints and marrow; It judges the thoughts and attitudes of the heart." (Hebrews 4:12). The Word of God is the power of God; by it, the universe was formed (Genesis 1:2). You cannot separate God from His Word. A lack of understanding of God's Word makes a believer ignorant of their right as a child of God. The Word of God is the manual of life. That's right! You can't survive this world as a believer without a good grasp of the Word of God. We are told in the book of Hosea 4:6 that God's people perish due to lack of knowledge. Knowledge of the Word of God is essential for every believer; you can't take advantage of what you don't know. Ignorance plays into the hand of the devil.

The Bible is the ultimate book for believers. The book of John 8:32 puts it this way "Then you will know the truth, and the truth will set you free." It's not your emotions that set you free. Nor is it the number of years that you have served God. Your theology degree is not capable of setting you free either. The only thing capable of setting you free according to the Bible is the Word of God. "God is spirit, and his worshipers must worship in the Spirit and in truth." (John 4:24).

Asking God for what He has already given us will only lead to frustration, discouragement, and unbelief on our part. Believers are supposed to live by every Word that comes from the mouth of God (Matthew 4:4). "God is not human, that he should lie, not a human being, that he should change his mind. Does he speak and then not act? Does he promise and not fulfill?" (Numbers 23:19).

Take salvation, for instance. Christ became the atonement for our sin. This was a one-time sacrifice for us, meaning salvation is available for everyone. Still, we have to play our parts to receive it. Christ has done His part, and the rest is left to us. We have to accept the finished work of the cross if we want to partake in this gift. We will not spend our time praying and hoping that Christ will someday remember us in His infinite mercy. Ignorance of how to receive the finished work can prevent us from getting saved. Say we decide to wait until God shows up in our dreams to perform a special atonement for us. We will be in this position for a very long time. Why? Because that's not the way to go about it. The Bible clearly states that we must accept the finished work of the cross for us to be called God's children.

The same concept can be applied to healing. Healing is part of the finished work of the cross; here is what the Bible has to say about this in the book of Isaiah 53:4–5, "Surely he took up our pain and bore our suffering, yet we considered him punished by God, stricken by him, and afflicted. But he was pierced for our transgressions, he was crushed for our iniquities; the punishment that brought us peace was on him, and by his wounds, we are healed."

This Bible passage clearly states that Jesus took our place on the cross; every punishment that was meant for us was placed on Him so that you and I can be free from the curse of the law. Sickness and disease have no place in the life of a believer. We, believers, have overcome sickness in Christ Jesus. Here is what the Bible has to say about this, in the book of Isaiah 53:11, "After he has suffered, he will see the light of life and be satisfied; by his knowledge, my righteous servant will justify many, and he will bear their iniquities."

The above passage tells us that God the Father shall be satisfied whenever we come to Him in the name of His Son because He shall see the labor of His soul and be satisfied by it. It goes on to say that by His knowledge, many shall be justified because He shall bear their iniquities. The abundant grace that we have today as believers are borne out of God's love for us. Sickness has nothing against us because we have been set free by the One who has the power to judge. Here is what the Bibles says in the book of Romans 8:31–32, "What, then, shall we say in response to these things? If God is for us, who can be against us? He who did not spare his own Son but gave him up for us all—how will he not also, along with him, graciously give us all things?"

If the One who has the power to justify and condemn died for you and me, who can bring charges against you (spiritually, that is)? Deuteronomy 28:14–68 talks about the calamities that will befall us if we fail to obey God's commandments, and in Romans 6:14, the Bible tells us that sin shall no longer be our master because we are not under the law but grace. This confirms what was written in Galatians 3:13–14, "Christ redeemed us from the curse of the law by becoming a curse for us, for it is written: "Cursed is everyone who is hung on a pole. "He redeemed us in order that the blessing given to Abraham might come to the Gentiles through Christ Jesus so that by faith we might receive the promise of the Spirit."

If we believe we are under grace as it is written in the Word of God, then Deuteronomy 28:1–13 is our portion. We ought to be bold enough to command sickness to leave our bodies and those of our loved ones in Jesus' name because sickness does not have a legal right to torment us. This is not to say that it is okay for us to consume foods that are deemed unhealthy or harmful. Nor is it okay for us to abuse our body. Here is how the Bible explains God's ownership of our body in the book of 1 Corinthians 6:19-20, "Do you not know that your bodies are temples of the Holy Spirit, who is in you, whom you have received from God? You are not your own; you were bought at a price. Therefore, honor God with your bodies."

That's right, our body belongs to God, and as such, we should treat it as God's property. If you believe that your body belongs to God and you know that the God whom you serve does not accept debased things, you should know that sickness is illegal and should never be tolerated. Stand on the Word of God, and command anything that does not glorify God in any way to leave your body in Jesus' name.

Let this sink in. Sickness has no legal right to ravage the life of a believer. Here is what the Word of God has to say about it in 1 Peter 2:24–25, "He himself bore our sins" in his body on the cross, so that we might die to sins and live for righteousness; "by his wounds, you have been healed."

For "you were like sheep going astray," but now you have returned to the Shepherd and Overseer of your souls."

We should never forget that Jesus Christ is our healer (Psalm 107:20) and that healing is part of our benefits (Psalm 103:3). As a child of God, you should not beg God for something He has freely given you; doing so constitutes ignorance. Remember that ignorance of the Word of God is why His people suffer (Hosea 4:6). The Bible tells us in the book of John 10:10, "The thief comes only to steal and kill and destroy; I have come that they may have life, and have it to the full." According to the Bible, the thief is none other than the devil.

Not spending quality time on God's Word will allow the enemy to sell a counterfeit doctrine to us, the consequences of which can be dire. The Word of God is what builds our faith. Here is what the Bible has to say about faith in Romans 10:17, "Consequently, faith comes from hearing the message, and the message is heard through the Word about Christ." Without the Word, we will never build the necessary faith to receive from God and keep the enemy away.

Chapter 3

Hindrances to the Manifestation of God's Divine Blessings

Absence of the Fear of God

If the fear of God is to eschew evil because evil is contrary to the nature of God, then the absence of the fear of God means that believers do things as it pleases them. God is no longer the driving factor in their decision-making. Decisions are made based on their understandings and needs. Faith is not applied in their daily lives because the five senses are now the defector driver for decision-making. This attitude can easily pull a believer away from God's blessings, or in some cases, hinder God's blessings from manifesting in their lives.

A believer who does not exercise Godly fear is bound to make many mistakes in life. These mistakes can bring frustration, discouragement, confusion, and sometimes disappointment in our walk with God. You can never have a good relationship with God if you lack the fear of God. Doing things as it pleases you is a no-no in God's kingdom.

The fear of God is a must-have for every believer. There is no substitution for this. The absence of the fear of God means that God is not our shepherd (Psalm 25:12). This goes against the biblical doctrine. Take forgiveness, for instance. It will be tough for you to forgive someone who knowingly wronged you. The human way of dealing with this matter is quite different from God's way. Why? Because God is not a man, and His ways are quite different from ours. It is like comparing the distance between Heaven and earth. You can imagine what the difference would be. God is love, and His love knows no bounds. If you can't love your neighbor as yourself, it will be challenging for you to walk with God because our walk with Him is centered around love. God does not entertain malice, hatred, backbiting, jealousy, etc. The same cannot be said about humans.

Ignorance of the Word

We can't take advantage of what God has freely given us if we are ignorant of the Word. A believer who lacks a good grasp of the Word is like a soldier of the world's most powerful nation who lacks a basic knowledge/understanding of how to operate the state-of-the-art war equipment at his disposal. What do you think will be this soldier's fate when approached by an enemy soldier? The fact that he has the best weapons at his disposal will be of no use to him if he doesn't know how to use them.

This is precisely the case with many believers. Many of us do not know how to use the Word of God in times of need. We rely so much on other people while the most potent weapon is at our disposal. It is the truth and only the knowledge of the truth that can set us free.

Ignorance of the Word of God is why many believers move from church to church. In the end, many of them experience nothing but disappointment, discouragement, failure, and sometimes defeat. This ought not to be so. Jesus paid the ultimate price for us to live a life of abundance on earth. Naaman almost missed out on his healing due to his ignorance of who God was. If not for his servant, he would have gone back to his country with the same disease from which God wanted to deliver him. The instruction given to the commander of the army of the king of Syria was too easy, and as such, he despised it.

2 Kings 5:9–16,

"So Naaman went with his horses and chariots and stopped at the door of Elisha's house. Elisha sent a messenger to say to him, "Go, wash yourself seven times in the Jordan, and your flesh will be restored, and you will be cleansed."

But Naaman went away angry and said, "I thought that he would surely come out to me and stand and call on the name of the LORD his God, wave his hand over the spot and cure me of my leprosy. Are not Abana and Pharpar, the rivers of Damascus, better than all the waters of Israel? Couldn't I wash in them and be cleansed?" So, he turned and went off in a rage.

Naaman's servants went to him and said, "My father, if the prophet had told you to do some great thing, would you not have done it? How much more, then, when he tells you, 'Wash and be cleansed!" So he went down and dipped himself in the Jordan seven times, as the man of God had told him, and his flesh was restored and became clean like that of a young boy.

Then Naaman and all his attendants went back to the man of God. He stood before him and said, "Now I know that there is no God in all the world except in Israel. So please accept a gift from your servant."

The prophet answered, "As surely as the LORD lives, whom I serve, I will not accept a thing." And even though Naaman urged him, he refused."

The only way to overcome ignorance of the Word is to spend time on the Word of God. As you do so, ask the Holy Spirit, the author of the Word, to reveal the power and mysteries behind each Word to you. Everything we are looking for in life can be found in the Word of God. We grow in faith as we study the Word. The more you spend time on the Word, the more you grow spiritually. Make it a habit to read the Bible daily, just like God instructed Joshua to study and meditate on the book of the Law day and night. He was also instructed to observe and do all that is written in it for his way to be prosperous. (Joshua 1:8).

Lack of Faith

Here is how the Bible defines faith, "Now faith is confidence in what we hope for and assurance about what we do not see. This is what the ancients were commended for. By faith we understand that the universe was formed at God's command, so that what is seen was not made out of what was visible." (Hebrews 11:1–3). Faith is believing that God has answered our prayers after we've prayed according to His will. Faith is not praying over and over again on the same request. Faith is knowing that God will do what He says He will do and that He is able to do way beyond our ask, according to the power that works in us (Ephesians 3:20).

Faith is vital in our walk with God; faith in the Word of God is a must for every believer. According to the Bible, without faith, it is impossible to please God (Hebrews 11:6). The Word "impossible" means there is no alternative. Believers try to work around their lack of faith by having others pray for them, hoping that the faith of the One praying for them will compensate for their faithlessness. They forget that God cannot be mocked; whatsoever a man soweth, that shall he also reap (Galatians 6:7).

Here is a good analogy that will help shed more light on this subject; pharmaceutical companies manufacture drugs for a specific reason. These drugs are meant to be taken by humans whenever they feel unwell. After taking these drugs, the consumers don't have to contact the manufacturer to activate the drug in their system. Why? Because most drugs are designed to start working after being taken. All the consumers have to do is follow the directives of their primary care physician or the manufacture of the pharmaceutical drug, whichever is applicable.

Before any drug can be made available to the public, the manufacture of the said drug has to go through some rigorous approval process from a safety and efficacy perspective. End-user assurance is based on the fact that they know their government will not allow any drug into the market if it's deemed harmful to them or did not meet a defined criterion.

If we can have such faith in man-made drugs, how much more in the Word of God, which the Bible defined as living and powerful. After praying the Word of God, most Christians still find it difficult to believe that their prayer has been answered. It's as if we are waiting on the Lord to activate His Word in us. Can a living Word be activated? Remember what the Bible says about the Word of God in Isaiah 55:11, "so is my Word that goes out from my mouth: It will not return to me empty, but will accomplish what I desire and achieve the purpose for which I sent it." That's right! The Word of God will never return to Him empty. It must accomplish what God desired of it. We can take this Bible passage to the bank; God cannot lie; He will do whatever He said He would do. Manufactured drugs tend to fail us every now and then, but the same cannot be said of the living Word of God.

Our trust should always be in the infallible Word of God that can never fail and will never fail. The Bible states in Proverbs 30:5 that "Every Word of God is flawless; he is a shield to those who take refuge in him."

The story of the bronze serpent in the Bible (Numbers 21: 1-9) is a perfect example of the living Word of God in action. The story goes like this: God granted the Israelites their request against their enemy (Canaan), who initially took some of them as prisoners after defeating them in a battle. It wasn't long afterward that Israel decided to sin against God by speaking ill against Him and Moses when their soul was discouraged.

God, in His judgment, sent fiery serpents among the people, many of whom were bitten by the serpents; some died as a result of this. God instructed Moses to make a fiery serpent after the people repented from their sins. The serpent was to be placed on a pole. According to God's directives, anyone who is bitten shall live when he looks at it. Moses did as instructed by the Lord, and the lives of those bitten and were able to look on the bronze serpent were saved.

One key thing to note from this story is that the Obedience to God's Word restored the people; the Word of God became active the moment it went forth. The obedience to God's Word produced healing. It wasn't the bronze serpent that healed them but rather the living Word of God. Obedience to the Word of God is paramount, as we saw in the story of Naaman. Here is how the Bible describes the Word of God in the book of Jeremiah 23:29, "Is not my Word like fire," declares the Lord, "and like a hammer that breaks a rock in pieces?"

Pride

Pride can become a massive hindrance if not dealt with. Pride is something that God hates. Prideful people believe they are what they are today because of their efforts. They fail to give glory to God; it's all about them. They forget that they came into this world with nothing and that they will go back with nothing. According to the Bible, "The earth is the LORD's, and everything in it, the world, and all who live in it; for he founded it on the seas and established it on the waters." (Psalm 24:1–2).

Here is the list of things that God hates according to Proverbs 6:16–19: "There are six things the LORD hates, seven that are detestable to him: haughty eyes, a lying tongue, hands that shed innocent blood, a heart that devises wicked schemes, feet that are quick to rush into evil, a false witness who pours out lies and a person who stirs up conflict in the community." In Proverbs 18:12, the Bible tells us that "Before a downfall the heart is haughty, but humility comes before honor." And finally, we are told in James 4:6 that God resists the proud but grace is made available to the one with a humble heart. I don't think any believer will like to be opposed by God. The only way you and I can prevent God from resisting us is to humble ourselves before Him at all times. Humility is a must for any child of God who desires to live a life of abundance on earth.

Conclusion

God's desire is for every believer to partake in His divine blessings; there is no such thing as a unique formula. God's gifts are not for sale. He made them available to us according to the good pleasure of His will. Believers need to surrender it all to God for His divine blessings to manifest in their lives.

The story of Ruth comes to mind as someone whose attitude we ought to emulate if we are to experience everything the Lord has purposed for us on earth. Ruth gave up her life to follow her mother-in-law back to Israel. Naomi, Ruth's mother-in-law, unsuccessfully tried to dissuade Ruth from going back with her. Here is Ruth's response when asked by Naomi to return with her sister-in-law Orpah, "But Ruth replied, "Don't urge me to leave you or to turn back from you. Where you go, I will go, and where you stay, I will stay. Your people will be my people and your God my God. Where you die, I will die, and there I will be buried. May the LORD deal with me, be it ever so severely, if even death separates you and me." (Ruth 1:16–17).

Ruth's decision to forgo her own needs and follow her mother-in-law ushered her into a life of glory and honor. It didn't happen overnight, but it all started when she decided to follow her mother-in-law. Little did she know that her action would bring her under the covering of God Almighty.

Jesus is looking for such people today, that is, those who will forgo everything to follow Him. Here is what Jesus said regarding this, "Then Jesus said to his disciples, "Whoever wants to be my disciple must deny themselves and take up their cross and follow me. For whoever wants to save their life will lose it, but whoever loses their life for me will find it." (Matthew 16:24–25).

God's blessings are already inside us. We need to quit chasing God's blessings and start living the life that God has called us into, which is a life of freedom. If God gave up His Son to become an everlasting sacrifice for us, why shouldn't He give us all things through Him?

Related Bible Passages

Blessings

Proverbs 10:22; Ezekiel 34:26; Exodus 23:25; Jeremiah17:7–8; Proverbs 16:3; Jeremiah 29:11; Psalm 119:2; 2 Corinthians 9:8; Proverbs 10:7; Deuteronomy 15:6, Joshua 1:8; Proverbs 2:7; Psalm 33:12; Leviticus 26:3–4, Proverbs 11:25; Psalm 32

Believe

Acts 13:38–39; Mark 1:15; 1 Timothy 1:16; John 14:1; John 3:36; John 6:29; John 11:25–26; Acts 16:31; John 1:12; Mark 11:23, 24; James 1:6, John 11:40;

Faith

2 Corinthians 5:7; 1 John 5:4; James 2:17; Matthew 17:20; Hebrews 11:11; Matthew 21:21; Galatians 5:6; Ephesians 2:8–9; 1 Timothy 6:12; Hebrews 12:2; 1 Timothy 5:8

Healing

Luke 4:18; Matthew 10:8; Luke 10:9; Luke 8:50; Mark 10:52; Matthew 8:16–17; Psalm 146:8; James 5:14–15; 2 Chronicles 7:14; Exodus 15:26; Proverbs 3:7–8

Righteousness

Proverbs 14:34; Proverbs 11:4; Psalm 33:5; Matthew 5:6; Psalm 31:1; 1 Timothy 6:11; Psalm 103:17–18; Isaiah 61:10; Titus 3:5; Isaiah 41:10; Isaiah 54:17

Trust

Jeremiah 17:7–8, Proverbs 29:25; Psalm 13:5–6; Isaiah 26:3; Psalm 91:1–2; Psalm 37:5–6; Psalm 143:8; Psalm 9:10; Psalm 118:8

Word

Psalm 119:105; Psalm 119:11; Psalm 130:5; Psalm 18:30; John 1:14; Isaiah 55:11; Psalm 143:8; Psalm 119:160; Galatians 5:14; Proverbs 16:20; Ezekiel 12:28; Jeremiah 23:29; Deuteronomy 4:2; Ezekiel 37:4–6

Printed in the United States
by Baker & Taylor Publisher Services